MICHEL ROUX

vinaigrettes & chilled sauces

Dedication

To my son Alain, who cooks side-by-side with me at The Waterside Inn.

Contents

Red Pepper Butter on

toast canapés (page 59)

Foreword

In the 1960s, during my 'Rothschild years', when I worked in Paris for the banking family, Mademoiselle Cécile de Rothschild and her close friends enjoyed coming home from the theatre to a cold buffet supper, particularly in May and June, the Parisian 'high season'. She and her guests always admired my appetising display of cold dishes before tasting them; each dish was served with its own chilled sauce creating a perfect harmony with the food. It was like a festival of sauces, providing new enjoyment at each one of these suppers. In order to surprise her each time, I had to be constantly inventive. Small lobsters or langoustines, piled high on a platter and dressed with a Sauce Vierge were one of my original creations, which has become a classic. Cold fillets of beef studded with pork fat and truffles, and surrounded by finely diced spring vegetables were served with a Remoulade Sauce, while my Green Sauce accompanied a magnificent cold poached salmon. I was not allowed to glaze fish with even a hint of aspic, because my employer believed that it would spoil the flavour of the salmon and the sauce. And there were always mountains of white asparagus; she liked these served barely warm and would drown them with generous spoonfuls of Gribiche Sauce. None of her guests ever refused a sauce. "Chef", they would say, "it's your sauce which adds flavour to a dish and gives it a new dimension." And then they would add, "you see what I mean, Chef". Such happy memories!

Now that I am well into my fifties, once or twice a week I treat myself to a frugal meal of salad, fish or cold meats. I feel I owe it to my liver; every Frenchman is a hypochondriac and I am no exception! But a light repast is not necessarily a boring one - quite the reverse. I spend a few minutes giving my imagination free rein to mentally compose my plate of salad. I prefer crunchy leaves to tender lettuces; escarole, lambs' lettuce, radicchio, frisée and dandelion are among my favourites. I prefer garden salads to those grown under glass, which I find rather sad and tasteless.

After a few moments' thought, I prepare one of my vinaigrettes; my final choice depends on my mood and the salad the dressing is to accompany. Parmesan or Roquefort Vinaigrette go well with crisp leaves; Truffle Vinaigrette is particularly good with frisée, while Maman Roux's Vinaigrette is perfect with escarole. I mix in some fresh herbs from my garden; tarragon and parsley are two of my favourites. Finally, I give my salad a festive air, enhancing it with colourful edible flowers like nasturtiums or geraniums. I cast an approving eye over the finished dish. My mouth begins to water. I grab a piece of crusty bread and tuck into my appetising salad. The simplest salad can be unbelievably delicious if it is well thought out and, of course, dressed with an excellent vinaigrette.

Some days, I want nothing more than a big bowl of vegetable soup or simply a home-made sandwich. On Mondays, when The Waterside Inn is closed, I enjoy this even more, especially when my wife Robyn prepares me a plate of sandwiches whose delicious aroma fills the house. They often consist of freshly toasted country bread, generously filled with thin slices of cold meat or ham, lightly cooked eggs or assorted raw vegetables. Robyn always adds a dollop of the excellent cold sauces, which she can whip up much faster than I can.

Cold sauces are magical; they are the ideal partners for any occasion. Quick and easy to prepare, they accompany and enhance to perfection any dish, from the simplest to the most complex.

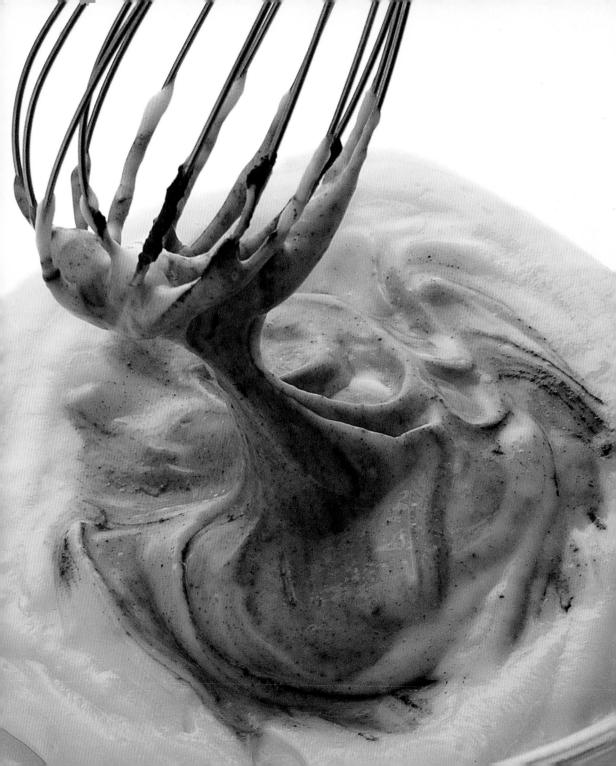

About Sauces

- Chilled sauces and vinaigrettes are light and refreshing – the perfect complement to summer dishes and starters. Many are light, low in calories and kind to the digestion; most are quick and easy to prepare.
- All sauces, however simple or complex, should be based on good-quality ingredients. Aromatics, fresh herbs, spices and wines must be chosen with the utmost care. Remember that it is vital to get the proportions precisely right. Ingredients with a very strong flavour (pungent spices, herbs and spirits, for example) should be used in moderation.
- Just as you would choose the finest seasonal ingredients for a finished dish, you should always make your sauces with the best of the season's produce. The end result will be full of flavour and absolutely delicious.
- Preparation times given in this book are based on ingredients which have been weighed out and prepared as indicated in the ingredients list. They do not include the time taken to peel or chop vegetables, soften butter, etc.
- Thin sauces can be strained straight through a conical sieve. Thicker sauces should be pushed through the sieve by pressing with the back of a ladle or twisting a small whisk.

About Vinaigrettes, Chilled Sauces and Flavoured Butters

Chilled sauces and vinaigrettes

A good sauce or vinaigrette can make the difference between an ordinary dish or salad and one which is exceptional. A sauce should provide a contrast of texture and flavour to the dish with which it is served, but it must always complement the dish, not overpower it.

The sauces in this book are almost all easy to prepare and very few need any particular culinary knowledge or skill. All that is required is a little care, so anyone can conjure up a delicious chilled sauce or vinaigrette with ease.

Emulsion sauces: Emulsion sauces are refined, delicate and unctuous. One of my favourites is mayonnaise, a wonderful eggy creation, which forms the basis for many other sauces. It is delicious served with any cold poached or roast chicken, cold fish and seafood, or poached fish like salmon, hake or cod. It can be enriched with double cream, or lightened with whipped cream, yoghurt or fromage blanc.

Many cold emulsion sauces are prepared with raw eggs. Where possible, I recommend that you use pasteurised eggs, although if you can only find these in dried form, they are obviously not suitable for mayonnaise and its derivatives. If you use fresh eggs, make sure they are free-range and come from a reliable source. Do not serve sauces made with raw eggs to people who may be particularly at risk, such as the elderly, the very young, or pregnant women.

Always serve emulsion sauces in a porcelain or stainless steel sauceboat. Never use silver, as the sauce will tarnish the metal and can quickly oxidize.

Flavoured butters

Flavoured butters are tasty, simple to prepare and come in a range of attractive colours, from pastel to vibrant, depending on their composition. They can be used instead of a sauce (allow 30 g per person) and as a topping for vegetables or poached, pan-fried or grilled fish and meat.

I usually roll the butters into a sausage shape, using cling film, but if you prefer, they can be piped into rosettes using a piping bag with a fluted nozzle. Many make delicious canapés; soften the butter slightly and spread or pipe it on to toasted croûtons.

The butters are at their most flavoursome made just before serving and firmed up for a few minutes in the fridge, but they can be kept refrigerated for three or four days, or frozen for several weeks. That way, you can always add extra flavour to a dish in a matter of moments.

I use my flavoured butters to enhance a sauce, to refine it (with foie gras butter, for example) or to personalize it as the mood takes me with the flavour of vegetables, herbs or shellfish. This book contains my particular favourites, but you can create dozens of other butters, using mustard, olives, truffles, tomato ... let your imagination run riot.

Vegetable Butter (page 60)

served on boiled new potatoes

Basic Ingredients

Herbs, spices and flavourings

This subject deserves an entire encyclopaedia to do it justice instead of just a few lines. But since this is a book about sauces, I shall mention only those herbs and spices which are familiar to me and which I use to flavour and enhance my own cooking.

In Bray, I have created a herb garden on the banks of the Thames. Every day in the summer months, I painstakingly and parsimoniously pick the numerous different herbs I need for my sauces and salads. Freshness is a vital factor in the success of a sauce and my herb garden is my trump card.

If you use dried herbs, keep them in airtight jars in a cool, dark place. Spices lose their colour and flavour if they are kept too long; you should throw away any open ones after 3 to 6 months because they will add nothing to your sauces, and may even spoil them.

The golden rules for using herbs and spices:

• Use small quantities but good quality
• Do not mix contradictory and powerful flavours

If you obey these rules, you will discover a wonderful world of flavours – subtle, complex, musky, fresh, spicy and delectable.

Fines herbes are a mixture of fresh herbs in equal quantities: chervil, chives, parsley and tarragon. They should be snipped, not chopped, preferably only a short time before using so that they retain the maximum flavour and do not become bitter.

The most popular culinary herbs are: basil, bay leaf, chervil, chives, fresh coriander, dill, fennel, garlic, horseradish, lavender, lemon grass, lemon verbena, lovage, marjoram, mint, oregano, flat or curly parsley, rosemary, sage, savory, sorrel, tarragon and thyme.

The most popular spices are: caraway, cardamom, cayenne, cinnamon, cloves, coriander seeds, cumin, curry, five-spice, ginger, juniper, mace, nutmeg, pepper (black, green, white and pink), paprika, pimento, poppy seeds, saffron and star anise.

Garlic: Always halve garlic cloves lengthways and remove the green shoot from the middle, which can be bitter and indigestible.

Vegetable essences: These are used to lighten a sauce which is over-rich, powerful or too thick, or to add a more aromatic flavour to a sauce or vegetable court-bouillon. They can also be served separately in a ramekin to accompany steamed fish, or stirred warm into a vinaigrette to serve with vegetables or shellfish.

Vegetable essences can be made with almost any kind of vegetables and herbs. Chop them finely or coarsely, depending on their structure, place in a pan with a very small amount of liquid (water or chicken stock). Cover and cook until tender, then strain through a fine-mesh conical sieve and keep in a small airtight jar.

Vinegar and lemon: A few drops of vinegar or lemon juice added to a characterless sauce just before serving will pep up the taste.

Dairy products

These play an extremely important part in making cold sauces and flavoured butters.

Crème fraîche: This slightly acidulated cream is light and refreshing and is delicious added to most cold sauces. It is available in full- and low-fat versions.

Double cream: This is used as a liaison, but above all it makes sauces rich and velvety.

Fromage blanc and fromage frais: These are the champions of low-calorie sauces; you can even buy virtually fat-free versions. They are perfect for summer sauces, but their neutral taste demands the addition of herbs, spices or other flavourings.

Roquefort: My noble Lord Roquefort acquires star status in salad dressings and cold sauces to go with crudités. I adore the way that, used in moderation, it creates an explosion of different taste sensations in a sauce. Bleu d'Auvergne and fourme d'Ambert can be used instead, but they cannot equal the real thing.

Unsalted butter: I only ever use unsalted butter in my cooking. For me, it is the finest of all dairy products. It is natural and healthy and practically indispensable in the kitchen. Its delicate taste and different complexities vary according to its provenance and origins. At The Waterside Inn, the butter I have chosen is the appellation contrôlée Echiré from the Deux-Sèvres, which is unbeatable for quality and value. It is available in good supermarkets.

Yoghurt: I use tiny quantities of plain yoghurt to add a touch of acidity to certain sauces, particularly those for fish. I use it often in a number of my low-calorie summer vinaigrettes.

Oils and vinegars

The most popular oils are: olive, groundnut, sunflower, corn, rape seed, hazelnut, walnut, sesame, grapeseed and safflower. Some highly-scented oils, like walnut or hazelnut, need to be diluted with a flavourless oil. Use one part flavoured oil to two parts groundnut oil. These oils and vinegars form the basis for every kind of vinaigrette, together with emulsifiers such as cream, yoghurt, fromage blanc, mustard and other refreshing condiments.

Vinegars: The vinegars I tend to use most frequently are: red wine, white wine, sherry, balsamic, champagne, fruit such as raspberry or blackcurrant (home-made is best), tarragon, cider and garlic-flavoured wine vinegar.

I have included a recipe for Fruit Vinegar. You do not need one for tarragon vinegar: simply immerse a few sprigs of tarragon in a bottle of white wine vinegar and leave it for several weeks to perfume and flavour the vinegar.

Le Vezou: I discovered this unusual and little-known vinegar on one of my many visits to Martinique. Made from pure cane sugar, it is 100% natural. The first alcoholic fermentation produces cane sugar wine, which is then acetified and fermented for about four months. The liquid is clarified and filtered to become a beautiful pale amber, gently acidulated vinegar with a slightly fruity flavour which sets it apart from other vinegars. I use it for deglazing in some of my sauces for pigeon, duck and calves' liver. It also makes the perfect vinaigrette for delicate salads and for dressing asparagus. This delicious vinegar is made by the La Mauny Vallée Company, which is famous for its rum production.

Recipes

- Vinaigrettes are used to dress all kinds of salads from tender green leaves to robust, crunchy vegetables. They are also used for hors d'oeuvres – crudités, gourmand salads made with thinly-sliced raw or smoked fish, seafood, baby vegetables, asparagus tips, mange-tout and mushrooms. They even marry well with certain fruits, like citrus, apples and raspberries.
- Take care never to combine conflicting colours and textures, and do not use too many ingredients which will detract from or spoil the fine flavour of the principal ingredient. By all means be creative, but keep your imagination under control.
- Vinaigrettes are all the better for being prepared a few minutes in advance, as they will lose some of their savour and aroma if you make them too long before using them.
- Vegetable coulis are extremely useful and taste wonderful. They are champion sauces, light, insubstantial and quick to prepare. You can combine two or three on a plate and eat them with a teaspoon.
- Included in this book are some very quick recipes which require virtually no cooking. They are light, low in calories and kind to the digestion. They are perfect for salads, cruditiés and vegetables. You could devise many others using the same simple principles.

Basil Vinaigrette

Use this vinaigrette with fresh pasta, green beans and potato salad.

Ingredients:

6 tbsp olive oil
2 tbsp red wine vinegar
15 g basil leaves, snipped
1 small garlic clove, finely chopped
30 g shallot, finely chopped
40 g very ripe tomatoes
Salt and freshly ground pepper

Serves 6

Preparation time: 5 minutes

Put all the ingredients in a blender and whizz for 30 seconds.
Season to taste with salt and pepper.

Parmesan Vinaigrette

This dressing goes well with raw chicory, spinach or sliced mushrooms. If it seems too thick, thin it with a little vegetable stock or warm water.

Ingredients:

1 tsp English mustard powder
2 tbsp champagne vinegar
6 tbsp double cream
30 g freshly grated parmesan
1 tbsp snipped chives
Salt and freshly ground pepper

Serves 6

Preparation time: 5 minutes

In a bowl, stir the mustard powder into the vinegar,
then add the other ingredients and season.

Roquefort Vinaigrette

I enjoy this dressing in winter served with bitter leaves like dandelion, frisée or escarole. It is also good with crisply cooked French beans served warm and tossed in the vinaigrette just before serving.

Ingredients:

Serves 6

3 tbsp walnut oil

3 tbsp safflower or sunflower oil

2 tbsp tarragon vinegar

50 g roquefort, crushed with a fork

1 tsp snipped tarragon leaves

A few drops of worcestershire sauce

Salt and freshly ground pepper

Preparation time: 5 minutes

Combine all the ingredients in a bowl and mix together with a small whisk.

Lavender Vinaigrette

The flavours of lavender and honey subtly flavour this vinaigrette, which is excellent with raw sliced mushrooms or cucumber, or with tender salad leaves.

Ingredients:

Serves 6

Flowers from a stalk of not-too-flowery fresh lavender

3 tbsp groundnut oil

3 tbsp olive oil

2 tbsp white wine vinegar

1 tsp runny honey

Leaves from a sprig of thyme

Salt and freshly ground pepper

Preparation time: 5 minutes

Put all the ingredients in a blender and whizz for 30 seconds. Season to taste with salt and pepper.

Crustacean Oil

This wonderfully delicate oil is one of my favourites. It makes a superb dressing for fantasy seafood salads or warm asparagus spears (left).

Makes about 1 litre
Preparation time: 20 minutes, plus 3 hours' drying
Sterilization time: 35 – 45 minutes

Ingredients:

1 kg langoustines or crayfish,
cooked in salted water
1/2 head of garlic, unpeeled
1 sprig of thyme
2 bay leaves
1 small bunch of tarragon
1 tsp whole white peppercorns
1/2 tsp whole coriander seeds
Approximately 1 L groundnut or olive oil
Salt

Special equipment:

a 1 – 1.5 L kilner jar. Ideally, this should be new – if not, it must be scrupulously clean

Preheat the oven to 120°C/250°F/gas mark 1/2. Remove the eyes of the crustaceans and separate the heads, claws and tails. Keep the tails to use as a garnish for fish or serve in a salad as an hors d'oeuvre. Roughly chop the heads and claws with a chef's knife, put them in a roasting pan and place in the oven to dry for 3 hours. Put the dried heads and claws into the kilner jar with the aromatics, fill up with oil to within 2 cm of the top and seal the lid carefully.

To sterilize the oil, you will need a saucepan at least as tall as the jar. Line the bottom and sides of the pan with foil; this will protect the glass, which might explode if it should knock against the side of the pan. Put in the jar and pour in enough water, salted with 300 g salt per litre of water, to come up to the level of the oil in the jar, but not to submerge it. Bring the water to the boil over high heat and boil for 35 – 45 minutes, depending on the size of the kilner jar.

After sterilization, leave the jar at room temperature until completely cold, then refrigerate for at least 8 days before using the oil. It will keep for months in the sealed sterile jar if stored in a cool place. Once opened, decant the oil into a bottle; it will keep for several weeks in the fridge.

Crustacean Oil Vinaigrette

I serve this vinaigrette at The Waterside Inn with a little dish of freshly cooked noodles and mixed shellfish – a veritable feast! It is also remarkably good served with poached lobster.

Ingredients:

100 ml Crustacean Oil (opposite)
1 tbsp wholegrain mustard
Juice of 1 lemon
1 tbsp snipped tarragon leaves
Salt and freshly ground pepper

Serves 6

Preparation time: 5 minutes

In a bowl, whisk all the ingredients together and season to taste with salt and pepper.

Tea Vinaigrette

This light, refreshing dressing is perfect for a simple green salad. Choose the variety of tea according to your taste.

Ingredients:

3 tbsp white wine vinegar
2 tsp Ceylon tea leaves
120 ml sunflower oil
1 tbsp snipped flat-leaf parsley
Salt and freshly ground pepper

Serves 6

Preparation time: 5 minutes, plus cooling time

Cooking time: about 2 minutes

In a small saucepan, bring the vinegar to the boil and immediately add the tea. Turn off the heat, cover the pan, leave to cool for 10 minutes, then strain through a wire-mesh conical sieve into a bowl. Mix in the other ingredients with a spoon and season to taste.

Saffron Vinaigrette

This vinaigrette is especially delicious served with a mixed salad of tender leaves like lambs' lettuce or oak leaf lettuce garnished with scallops or warm grilled langoustine tails and a few coriander leaves.

Ingredients:

3 tbsp white wine vinegar
A generous pinch of saffron threads
6 tbsp groundnut oil
1 tbsp sesame oil
1 tsp soy sauce
Salt and cayenne pepper

Serves 6

Preparation time: 5 minutes

In a small saucepan, warm the vinegar, add the saffron, turn off the heat and infuse until cold. Whisk in all the other ingredients. The vinaigrette is now ready to serve.

Beer Vinaigrette

Serve this vinaigrette with cured tongue, ham or cold sausages like cervelat or a lightly smoked coarse pork morteau. It is also excellent served with barely warm steamed leeks.

Ingredients:

100 ml light beer
30 g shallots, chopped
50 ml white wine vinegar
150 ml groundnut oil
Salt and freshly ground pepper

Serves 6

Preparation time: 5 minutes

Cooking time: 5 minutes

Pour the beer into a small saucepan, set over high heat and reduce to 2 tablespoons.

Delicately mix in all the other ingredients, adding salt and pepper to taste. Refrigerate the vinaigrette until needed.

Tomato Vinaigrette

Use this refreshing and delectable vinaigrette to enliven a fresh pasta salad or or boiled rice. If you prefer, replace the coriander with double the quantity of basil leaves. If necessary, you can use canned or bottled tomato juice but the flavour will not be as fresh.

Ingredients:

150 ml tomato juice, freshly pressed
from very ripe tomatoes
50 ml olive oil
50 ml sherry vinegar
5 g snipped fresh coriander leaves
salt and cayenne pepper

Serves 6

Preparation time: 3 minutes

Put all the ingredients in a bowl and mix gently. Check the seasoning, which should be quite assertive. Keep the vinaigrette in the fridge until ready to use, but for no longer than 48 hours.

Low-calorie Vinaigrette

This flavoursome diet dressing marries well with most salads.

Ingredients:

1 tsp wholegrain mustard
Juice of 2 lemons
120 ml tomato juice, preferably
freshly pressed
25 g onion, finely chopped
2 tbsp olive oil
1 tbsp snipped basil or tarragon leaves
Salt and freshly ground pepper

Serves 6

Preparation time: 5 minutes

In a bowl, whisk together the mustard and lemon juice, then stir in all the other ingredients except the basil or tarragon; add this just before serving the vinaigrette.

❶

❷

Avocado Vinaigrette

This vinaigrette is excellent with any cold white meats, cold white fish or a salad of french beans. My favourite way to serve it is with barely warm poached or steamed cauliflower. If the sauce seems too thick, thin to a pouring consistency with a little more vinegar.

Ingredients:

1 ripe avocado

70 ml white wine vinegar

2 hard-boiled egg yolks, crushed with a fork

1 tbsp Dijon mustard

200 ml groundnut oil

1 small garlic clove, crushed and finely chopped

5 g chervil, snipped

5 g parsley, snipped

A small pinch of cayenne pepper

Salt and freshly ground pepper

Serves 6

Preparation time: 8 minutes

Halve the avocado and remove the stone (1). Peel the avocado, cut it into chunks and place in a bowl. Add the vinegar and mash together, using a fork, then mix in the hard-boiled egg yolks, still using the fork (2). (If you use a whisk throughout, the vinaigrette will emulsify and become more like a mayonnaise).

Add all the other ingredients and mix in first with a fork (3), then with a whisk (4). Check the seasoning, which should be quite assertive and not at all bland. Add salt and pepper to taste (5).

Pour the vinaigrette into a bowl (6) and serve as soon as possible. Do not keep it for longer than 6 – 8 hours, as it has a tendency to ferment.

Thai Vinaigrette

This refreshing vinaigrette is ideal for seasoning crisp salad leaves like cos lettuce or batavia. It makes an excellent dressing for cold cooked rice noodles. A few prawns, sesame seeds and some extra coriander leaves make it even more tempting.

Ingredients:

2 cm piece of lemon grass, finely chopped

15 g coriander leaves, finely shredded

10 g chives, finely snipped

2 tbsp Thai fish sauce

1 tsp soy sauce

200 ml sunflower oil

50 ml rice wine vinegar

Freshly ground black pepper

Serves 10

Preparation time: *5 minutes, plus 2 hours' infusing*

Mix all the ingredients together in a bowl, season with pepper to taste, cover with cling film and leave the vinaigrette to infuse for 2 hours before using it.

Garlic Vinaigrette

Cooked garlic is delicious and easy to digest. This vinaigrette with its delicate aroma is perfect for well-flavoured mixed salads. Adjust the quantity of garlic to suit your own taste.

Ingredients:

A handful of coarse cooking salt

6 fine plump garlic cloves

2 tbsp balsamic vinegar

3 tbsp groundnut oil

3 tbsp walnut oil

1 tbsp snipped chives

Salt and freshly ground pepper

Serves 6

Cooking time: *about 10 minutes*

Preheat the oven to 180°C/350°F/gas mark 4. Spread the coarse salt over a small roasting pan, arrange the garlic cloves on top and bake in the oven for 10 minutes. To check whether the garlic is cooked, insert the tip of a knife into the centre; it should not meet any resistance. Remove the garlic cloves and use a fork to squash them out of their skins, one at a time. Place them on a plate. Scrape the garlic purée into a bowl, add the vinegar and salt and pepper to taste and whisk until amalgamated, then whisk in the two oils. Just before serving, stir in the chives.

Salad of rice noodles and prawns, dressed with Thai Vinaigrette and coriander sprigs

Maman Roux's Vinaigrette

My mother's creamy vinaigrette has been a favourite of mine since childhood. It is excellent with garden lettuce and escarole.

Ingredients:

1 tbsp freshly grated horseradish
(bottled will do at a pinch)
Juice of 1 lemon
1 tbsp white wine tarragon vinegar
6 tbsp double cream
40 g shallots, finely chopped
1 tbsp snipped tarragon leaves
Salt and freshly ground pepper

Serves 6

Preparation time: 5 minutes

Whisk together the horseradish, lemon juice, vinegar and seasoning. Gently stir in the cream. If necessary, thin the sauce with 1/2 tablespoon warm water. Add the shallots and tarragon just before mixing the dressing into the salad.

Cucumber Vinaigrette

This sauce is particularly nice in summer, served with green beans cooked al dente, or thinly sliced button mushrooms.

Special equipment:

A mandoline or vegetable grater

Serves 4

Preparation time: 10 minutes

Ingredients:

250 g cucumber
60 g shallots, finely chopped
1 tsp snipped chives
1 tsp snipped tarragon
1 tsp snipped flat-leaf parsley or chervil
6 tbsp olive oil
2 tbsp rice wine vinegar
Salt and freshly ground pepper

Peel the cucumber with a potato peeler, halve it lengthways, scoop out the seeds, then slice it as thinly as possible on the mandoline or with the grater. Place in a bowl and add all the other ingredients, seasoning to taste with salt and pepper. Cover with cling film until needed.

Truffle Vinaigrette

This vinaigrette is divine with a salad of frisée or escarole, or with baby new potatoes, pasta or tender young leeks, cooked briefly, refreshed and served warm.

Ingredients:

6 tbsp olive oil
2 tbsp red wine vinegar
60 g black truffle, preferably raw, finely chopped
1/2 small garlic clove, very finely chopped
1 anchovy fillet, rinsed in cold water and very finely chopped
2 hard-boiled egg yolks, rubbed through a sieve or finely chopped
Salt and freshly ground pepper

Serves 6

Preparation time: 5 minutes

Combine all the ingredients except the egg yolks in a bowl and mix with a spoon. Season with salt and pepper and stir in the egg yolks just before serving.

Anchovy Vinaigrette

Serve pan-fried fillets of red mullet, bream or bass, or tender cooked artichokes with a drizzle of this anchovy vinaigrette.

Ingredients:

3 tbsp olive oil
1 garlic clove, finely chopped
75 ml vegetable stock
3 anchovy fillets, finely chopped
6 green olives, finely chopped
2 tbsp balsamic vinegar
Salt and freshly ground pepper

Serves 6

Preparation time: 5 minutes

Cooking time: about 5 minutes

In a small saucepan, heat the oil to about 50°C, add the garlic and infuse for 30 seconds. Add the stock and heat to 50 – 60°C. Turn off the heat, whisk in the other ingredients and season to taste. Serve tepid.

Citrus Vinaigrette

This vinaigrette is good with all salads, particularly winter salad leaves such as escarole, chicory, frisée and radicchio.

Ingredients:

Zest of 1 orange, cut into fine julienne
and blanched
Juice of the orange
1 tbsp caster sugar
1 tsp Dijon mustard
Zest of 1 lemon, cut into fine julienne
and blanched
Juice of the lemon
6 tbsp groundnut oil
1 tbsp finely snipped parsley
Salt and freshly ground pepper

Serves 6

Preparation time: *5 minutes*

Cooking time: *2 minutes*

Put the orange zest and juice and the sugar in a small saucepan and reduce by two-thirds over low heat. Keep at room temperature.

In a bowl, whisk together the mustard, lemon juice, and salt and pepper to taste. Whisk in the oil, then the reduced orange juice and zest. Just before serving, stir in the lemon zest and parsley.

Grapefruit Vinaigrette

This is the perfect dressing for asparagus, green beans, or artichoke hearts and bottoms. Finely snipped tarragon adds an extra special something to the vinaigrette.

Ingredients:

Juice of 1 medium grapefruit
Juice of 1 lemon
1 tsp Dijon mustard
150 ml groundnut oil
A pinch of caster sugar
1 tbsp snipped tarragon (optional)
Salt and freshly ground pepper

Serves 8

Preparation time: *8 minutes*

Combine all the ingredients in a bowl, season to taste and mix delicately with a whisk. If you are using tarragon, stir it in just before serving.

Use this vinaigrette within 24 hours, as the citrus juices tend to oxidize if kept for longer.

Chive-flavoured Oil

Drizzle this oil over grilled fish or add some to a vinaigrette to give a pronounced chive flavour.

Ingredients:
500 ml olive oil
50 g chives, snipped

Makes 500 ml
Preparation time: **5 minutes**
Cooking time: **about 5 minutes**

In a saucepan, heat the oil to about 80°C, add the chives and cover the pan. Immediately, turn off the heat and leave the oil to cool. Once cold, whizz in a blender for 30 seconds, then pass the oil through a wire-mesh conical sieve, pour into a bottle and cork it. It will keep for several days.

Chilli Pepper Oil

Use this oil to add spiciness and zing to pizzas or vinaigrettes.

Ingredients:
500 ml olive oil
50 g mild fresh red chilli, finely chopped
1 sprig of thyme
1 bay leaf
1 unpeeled garlic clove

Makes 500 ml
Preparation time: **5 minutes**
Cooking time: **about 5 minutes**

In a saucepan, heat the oil to about 80°C. Add all the other ingredients and cover the pan. Immediately turn off the heat and leave the oil to cool. Once cold, pass it through a wire-mesh conical sieve, then pour into a bottle and cork it.

Fruit Vinegar

The exceptionally fine aroma of this home-made vinegar makes the effort involved in preparing it well worth while. I usually make it with raspberries but it is also excellent made with blackberries or blackcurrants. Fruit vinegars make delicious dressings for modern gourmand salads made with shellfish, raw vegetables, asparagus, artichokes, etc. Best of all, they can be used to deglaze the pan juices of pan-fried or roast red meats and especially game; they add an intense and original depth of flavour to the sauce. If the fruit is not very sweet, increase the quantity of sugar by 10 – 15%. The precise amount of vinegar obtained will depend on how much juice the fruit contains (this can vary by up to 30%).

Ingredients:

1.5 kg very ripe raspberries, blackberries or blackcurrants

1.25 L white wine vinegar

130 g sugar lumps or granulated sugar

200 ml white denatured alcohol or cognac

Makes about 1 litre

Preparation time: **15 minutes, plus 48 hours' maceration**

Cooking time: **1 hour**

Put half the fruit in a non-metallic bowl, cover with vinegar (1), then cover the bowl with a tea towel or cling film and leave in a cool place for 24 hours. This is the first maceration.

After this time, place a fine-mesh sieve over a bowl and drain the first maceration of fruit (2), pressing very lightly with the back of a ladle to extract as much juice as possible without pushing through any pulp (3). You can use small quantities of the pulp in sauces for game, or simply throw it away. Add the remaining fruit to the extracted juice, then proceed as for the first maceration.

When the second 24 hours have elapsed, drain the fruit into a saucepan in the same way as before. Add the sugar and alcohol or cognac (4), and leave until the sugar has dissolved. Stand the pan on a sheet of greaseproof paper in a bain-marie filled with water, set over high heat and bring to the boil. Lower the heat so that the water is just bubbling gently and cook the vinegar for 1 hour, adding more water to the bain-marie if necessary. The temperature of the vinegar should remain at a constant 90°C throughout; it must not boil (hence the need for a bain-marie). While it is cooking, skim the surface as often as necessary.

Transfer the vinegar into a non-metallic bowl and leave in a cool place until cold. Strain it through a muslin-lined conical sieve and a funnel into a bottle and cork it. The vinegar is now ready to use, and will keep for 3 weeks in the fridge.

Bois Boudran Sauce

An excellent sauce for roast chicken or poussin, Bois Boudran Sauce can also be used to coat a salmon or lightly poached trout just before serving. I have loved this sauce ever since the days when I cooked for the Rothschild family.

Ingredients:

150 ml groundnut oil
50 ml wine vinegar
85 g tomato ketchup
1 tsp worcestershire sauce
5 drops of tabasco
100 g shallots, chopped
5 g chervil, finely snipped
5 g chives, finely snipped
20 g tarragon, finely snipped
Salt and freshly ground pepper

Serves 6

Preparation time: 5 minutes

Combine the oil, vinegar, a pinch of salt and three turns of the pepper mill in a bowl. Stir with a small whisk, then add the ketchup, worcestershire sauce, tabasco, chopped shallots and all the snipped herbs. Adjust the seasoning with salt and pepper and keep at room temperature; the sauce is ready to use right away, but it can also be kept in an airtight container in the fridge for 3 days.

Poached salmon with Bois Boudran Sauce

Piquant Fromage Blanc Sauce

This sauce is most agreeable served with a cold vegetable terrine or a warm pizza-style tomato and courgette tart.

Ingredients:

400 g fromage blanc, whichever fat
content you prefer

Seeds from 2 passion fruit, scooped out
with a spoon

4 tbsp raspberry-flavoured Fruit Vinegar,
home-made (page 28) or shop-bought

1 tbsp finely snipped lemon verbena

$^1/_2$ tbsp soft green peppercorns,
well drained and chopped

Salt and cayenne pepper

Serves 8

Preparation time: 5 minutes

Put all the ingredients in a bowl and mix together with a spoon.
Season with salt and plenty of cayenne.

Avocado Sauce

Serve this sauce as a dip for raw vegetables, such as carrots, cauliflower, cucumber or radishes, or with cold langoustines or cooked mussels.

Ingredients:

1 avocado, about 300 g, peeled & stoned

300 g plain yoghurt

2 tbsp snipped dill

2 tbsp lemon juice

1 tsp strong Dijon mustard

A small pinch of curry powder

Salt and freshly ground pepper

Serves 6

Preparation time: 5 minutes

Combine all the ingredients in a blender and whizz for 30 seconds.
Adjust the seasoning with salt and pepper.

Ravigote Sauce

This sauce gives an extra lift to offal such as lamb's or calf's brains, tongue, feet, head, etc. I also like to serve it with potatoes boiled in their skins; leave your guests to peel their own potatoes and dip them in the sauce as they eat.

Ingredients:

6 tbsp groundnut or sunflower oil

2 tbsp white wine vinegar

1 tbsp small capers

1 tbsp cornichons or small gherkins,

tbsp finely snipped fines herbes (page 10)

30 g onion, finely chopped

Salt and freshly ground pepper

Serves 6

Preparation time: *5 minutes*

Combine all the ingredients in a bowl and mix thoroughly.

Oregano and Sun-dried Tomato Sauce

This sun-dried tomato sauce makes an excellent accompaniment to grilled veal chops and tournedos, or robust grilled fish like tuna or monkfish.

Ingredients:

160 g sun-dried tomatoes in olive oil

180 g very ripe fresh tomatoes

200 ml chicken stock

40 ml balsamic vinegar

bsp fresh oregano leaves, finely chopped

Salt and freshly ground pepper

For the basil oil:

60 ml extra-virgin olive oil

10 g fresh basil leaves

Serves 8

Preparation time: *10 minutes*

Combine all the tomatoes, chicken stock and balsamic vinegar in the bowl of a food processor. Whizz for 2 minutes, then strain the sauce through a conical sieve into a bowl. Add the chopped oregano and season with salt and pepper.

To make the basil oil, put the oil and basil in the clean bowl of the food processor. Season to taste with salt and pepper and whizz for 2 minutes. Pour the oil straight into a bowl (do not strain it).

Serve the tomato sauce either tepid or cold, poured in a ribbon around the meat or fish, then sprinkled with a few drops of basil oil.

Pistou Sauce

Pistou smells as good as it tastes. Use it to perfume Mediterranean soups and steamed fish. Its powerful, intoxicating flavour also goes well with pasta.

Ingredients:

4 garlic cloves, peeled, halved and green shoot removed

20 basil leaves

100 g freshly grated parmesan

150 ml olive oil

Salt and freshly ground pepper

Serves 6

Preparation time: 10 minutes

In a small mortar, crush the garlic to a purée (1) with a pinch of salt (or use a blender). Add the basil and crush or blend to a homogeneous paste (2). Add the parmesan (3), then trickle in the olive oil in a steady stream, stirring continuously with the pestle, as though you were making mayonnaise (4). Work the sauce until smooth. Season to taste with salt and pepper. Use the pistou immediately, or transfer it to a bowl and cover with cling film. It will keep in the fridge for several days.

Pesto: If you add 30 g grilled or toasted pine kernels together with the basil, you will obtain Italian pesto, which has a firmer, richer consistency.

Sauce Vierge

I serve this sauce with lobster cappelletti, steamed fillets of red mullet and sea bass, and fresh pasta.

Ingredients:

200 ml olive oil

80 g tomatoes, peeled, deseeded and finely diced

Juice of 1 lemon

2 tbsp snipped basil leaves

1 tbsp snipped chervil leaves

1 garlic clove, finely chopped

6 coriander seeds, crushed

Salt and freshly ground pepper

Serves 6

Preparation time: 5 minutes

Combine the ingredients in a bowl, mix gently and season. Just before serving, warm the sauce to about 30 – 40ºC.

Marinated Cucumber Relish

I really enjoy this cucumber relish, which our young protégé Mark Prescott often serves at his pub, The White Hart at Nayland. It is delicious served with fish galantines and terrines or with gravadlax.

Ingredients:

For the marinated cucumbers
(prepare these 2 hours in advance)

1 kg cucumbers
150 g onions
1 green pepper
1 red pepper
1 red chilli
Salt

For the syrup:

500 ml tarragon-flavoured white wine vinegar
300 g soft light brown sugar
A small pinch of ground cloves
1 tsp turmeric
2 tsp mustard seeds
1 tsp fennel seeds

Makes 550 g

Preparation time: **about 10 minutes, plus 2 hours' marinating**

Cooking time: **about 1^1/$_2$ hours**

Prepare and marinate the cucumbers 2 hours in advance. Leave them unpeeled, but halve them lengthways, scoop out the seeds and slice the flesh very thinly. Peel and finely slice the onions. Peel the green and red peppers, remove the seeds and white membranes and cut the flesh into very fine julienne. Cut the chilli into very fine julienne. Put everything in a non-metallic bowl, add salt to taste and leave to marinate for 2 hours.

To make the syrup, put all the ingredients in a saucepan and bring slowly to the boil over low heat. Cook for about 45 minutes, until the syrup is thick enough to coat a wooden spoon and your finger leaves a clear trace when you run it down the back of the spoon.

Drain the marinated ingredients, press to eliminate as much liquid as possible, then add them to the syrup. Cook gently for 45 minutes, stirring occasionally with a wooden spoon, until the relish has a soft, melting jam-like consistency. Transfer it to an airtight jar and keep in a cool place until ready to use. It will keep in the fridge for several weeks.

Peach Chutney

Make this chutney in summer, when peaches are fresh and cheap. It is delicious served with terrines and pâtés, cold meats, and especially with cold chicken for a picnic.

Ingredients:

500 g peaches, preferably yellow, peeled, stoned and roughly cut into large dice

60 g cooking apple, peeled and grated

1/2 tsp salt

125 g very ripe tomatoes, peeled, deseeded and chopped

60 g onion, finely chopped

Zest of 1 lime, finely chopped

Juice of the lime

150 g caster sugar

1/2 tsp ground cinnamon

1/2 tsp ground nutmeg

1/2 tsp ground white pepper

1 garlic clove, crushed

10 g fresh ginger, finely chopped

150 ml white wine vinegar

70 g flaked almonds

Makes about 700 g

Preparation time: **25 minutes**

Cooking time: **about 1 hour 10 minutes**

Combine all the ingredients except the peaches in a thick-bottomed saucepan and bring to the boil over very low heat, stirring from time to time with a wooden spoon. Continue to cook for about 30 minutes, giving a stir every 10 minutes, until the mixture is jam-like and syrupy. Test by wiping your finger down the back of the spoon; it should leave a clear trace.

Add the peaches and cook very gently for another 40 minutes, stirring every 10 minutes. Transfer the chutney to a 750 ml kilner jar, leave to cool completely, then seal the jar. Keep in the fridge until needed (it will keep for several weeks).

Pear Chutney

This chutney is best left for a few days before you eat it. Serve it with cold meats, terrines, pâtés and game, or simply spread on a slice of toast.

Makes about 600 g
Preparation time: 30 minutes
Cooking time: about 1 hour 50 minutes

Ingredients:

375 g pears, peeled, cored and cut into large dice
60 g cooking apple, peeled and chopped
1/2 tsp salt
125 g very ripe tomatoes, peeled, deseeded and chopped
60 g onion, finely chopped
60 g sultanas
1 tbsp orange zest, coarsely chopped
Juice of 1 orange
150 g caster sugar
1/4 tsp ground cinnamon
1/4 tsp ground nutmeg
1/4 tsp cayenne pepper
15 g fresh ginger, finely chopped
150 ml white wine vinegar
A pinch of saffron powder or threads

Combine all the ingredients except the pears in a thick-bottomed saucepan and bring to the boil over very low heat, stirring from time to time with a wooden spoon (1). Continue to cook for about 1 hour, giving a stir every 10 minutes, until the mixture is jam-like and syrupy (2). Test by wiping your finger down the back of the spoon; it should leave a clear trace. Add the pears and cook very gently for another 40 minutes, stirring every 10 minutes (3). Using a funnel, transfer the chutney to a 500 ml kilner jar. Leave to cool completely, then seal the jar. Keep in the fridge until needed (it will keep for several weeks).

Cumberland Sauce

This sauce miraculously enhances the character of meats and terrines. Serve it cold with galantines and ballotines, pork pies or any cold poultry or game. The sauce tastes even better the day after it is made.

Serves 4

Preparation time: **10 minutes**

Cooking time: **20 minutes**

Ingredients:

1 medium shallot, finely chopped

4 tbsp wine vinegar, preferably red

12 white peppercorns, crushed

100 ml veal stock

50 ml ruby port

2 tbsp redcurrant jelly

1 tsp worcestershire sauce

juice of 1 orange

Zest of 1 lemon, blanched and cut into julienne

Salt

Combine the shallot, vinegar and peppercorns in a small saucepan and reduce by two-thirds over high heat (1). Add the veal stock, port (left), redcurrant jelly, worcestershire sauce and orange juice, quickly bring to the boil, then lower the heat and simmer gently for 20 minutes. Season with salt. Pass the sauce through a conical sieve into a bowl, cool, then refrigerate, as the sauce should be served very cold. Meanwhile, shred the lemon zest into fine julienne (2) and stir it into the sauce just before serving.

Adding the port to the sauce

Mayonnaise

Mayonnaise forms the basis for numerous other sauces. It is also delicious served just as it is with cold poached or roast chicken, cold crab, lobster and langoustines, or poached fish such as salmon, hake and cod; the list is endless.

If you prefer, you can replace some of the groundnut oil with olive oil, but do not use more than one-quarter, as olive oil has a very pronounced flavour. For a creamier mayonnaise, mix in 2 tablespoons double cream after adding the warm vinegar or cold lemon juice.

Serves 4

Preparation time: 5 minutes

Ingredients:

2 egg yolks

1 tbsp strong Dijon mustard

250 ml groundnut oil

1 tbsp white wine vinegar, warmed, or

1 tbsp cold lemon juice

Salt and freshly ground pepper

Lay a tea towel on the work surface and stand a mixing or salad bowl on the towel. In the bowl, combine the egg yolks, mustard and a little salt and pepper (1) and mix with a whisk (2). Pour in the oil in a thin, steady stream, whisking continuously (3). When it is all incorporated, whisk more vigorously for 30 seconds to make a thick, glossy mayonnaise, then add the hot vinegar or cold lemon juice (4). Adjust the seasoning with salt and pepper.

The mayonnaise can be kept at room temperature, covered with cling film, until ready to use. However, it is not wise to keep it for more than a few hours unless you use very fresh or pasteurized eggs.

The finished Mayonnaise should be thick and glossy

Low-calorie Mayonnaise

This low-fat mayonnaise can be used to accompany the same dishes as classic mayonnaise. It is refreshing and full of flavour and because it is very low in calories, it is ideal for those on a diet. If you wish, add some snipped chives, mint, tarragon or chervil to the mayonnaise just before serving.

Ingredients:

150 g fromage frais (whichever fat content you prefer)

1 egg yolk

1 tsp strong Dijon mustard

1 tsp white wine vinegar or lemon juice

Salt and freshly ground pepper

Serves 4

Preparation time: 3 minutes

Place all the ingredients in a mixing or salad bowl and whisk until completely homogeneous. Adjust the seasoning and serve.

Rémoulade Sauce

This piquant sauce is perfect for a cold buffet, with assorted cold meats or as a condiment for picnic food like pressed tongue and roast pork or chicken.

Ingredients:

1 quantity Mayonnaise (page 43)

40 g cornichons or gherkins, finely chopped

20 g capers, finely chopped

1 tbsp snipped flat-leaf parsley

1 tbsp snipped chervil

1 tbsp snipped tarragon

1 anchovy fillet, crushed with the flat of a chef's knife and finely chopped

1 tsp Dijon mustard, chilled

Salt and freshly ground pepper

Serves 6

Preparation time: 3 minutes

Put the mayonnaise in a bowl and mix in all the other ingredients with a spatula. Season to taste.

Aïoli

This sauce is excellent with salt cod, bouillabaisse (to replace the traditional Rouille, page 54), fish soups and innumerable Mediterranean vegetables. Potatoes do not figure in a classic aïoli, but I like the rustic, creamy quality they add to the sauce.

Ingredients:

180 g baked potato pulp, rubbed through a sieve and kept at room temperature

4 garlic cloves, peeled, green shoot removed, and crushed (page 10)

1 raw egg yolk

2 hard-boiled egg yolks, rubbed through a sieve

200 ml olive oil

A pinch of saffron threads, infused in 3 tbsp boiling water

Salt and cayenne pepper

Serves 8

Preparation time: 15 minutes

In a mortar, combine the potato pulp, garlic, raw and cooked egg yolks and a pinch of salt if you wish. Crush these ingredients with a pestle until well amalgamated, then start to trickle in the olive oil in a thin, steady stream, working the mixture continuously with the pestle. When about half the oil has been incorporated, add the saffron and the hot infusion, still mixing as you go. Trickle in the remaining oil, working it in with the pestle to make a smooth, homogeneous sauce. Season with a good pinch of cayenne and salt to taste.

Vegetable or Herb Essence

This mayonnaise-based green sauce is wonderful served with cold fish, including smoked trout and eel. The essence can be used in many other hot or cold sauces and adds a unique herby flavour.

Ingredients:

250 g leaf spinach, washed and stalks removed

10 g chervil, washed and stalks removed

30 g parsley, washed and stalks removed

15 g tarragon, washed and stalks removed

15 g chives

15 g shallot, peeled and thinly sliced

500 ml water

Special equipment:

A large square of butter muslin

Makes 100 g

*Preparation time: **40 minutes***

*Cooking time: **about 20 minutes***

You will need to make the vegetable essence in two batches. Put half the ingredients in a blender and whizz first at low speed for 1 minute, then for another 4 minutes at medium speed. Scrape the resulting purée into a bowl and repeat the process.

Stretch the muslin loosely over a saucepan and secure it with string to stop it slipping. Pour the purée on to the muslin and leave the liquid to filter through (1). When most of it has dripped into the pan, remove the string, fold up the edges of the muslin and twist gently to extract as much liquid as possible (2). Discard the herb purée and rinse the muslin in cold water.

Set the pan containing the bright green juice over low heat and bring to a simmer, stirring occasionally with a wooden spoon. Add a pinch of salt and, as soon as the liquid begins to tremble, turn off the heat. Stretch the muslin very loosely over a bowl and secure it with string as before, then delicately ladle the contents of the saucepan on to the muslin. Leave for a few minutes to drain well, then use a palette knife or spoon to scrape off the soft green purée from the surface of the muslin (3). Place this in a ramekin, pour a trickle of groundnut oil over the surface of the essence (4) and keep in a cool place until ready to use (it will keep in the fridge for several days).

Green Sauce

This mayonnaise-based green sauce is wonderful served with cold fish, including smoked trout and eel.

Ingredients:

1 quantity Mayonnaise (page 43)

Vegetable Essence (page 46), to taste

1 tbsp groundnut oil

Salt

Special equipment:

a large square of butter muslin

Serves 4

*Preparation time: **40 minutes***

*Cooking time: **about 20 minutes***

To make the green sauce, use a whisk to stir as much of the vegetable essence as you wish into the mayonnaise. The quantity will depend on your taste and how much herby flavour you desire.

Vincent Sauce

This sauce, which dates from the 18th century, remains very popular. It is perfect for a summer buffet and is often served with poached salmon, hake or turbot in aspic or a chaud-froid.

Ingredients:

¹/₂ quantity Green Sauce (above)

¹/₂ quantity Tartare Sauce (page 52)

Serves 6

*Preparation time: **5 minutes***

Mix the two sauces together with a whisk until thoroughly amalgamated.

Alicante Sauce

Alicante sauce is perfect with cold asparagus, but it should not be chilled before serving. I prefer paprika to cayenne for its colour and flavour, but the choice is yours. As always, once beaten egg whites have been added to the sauce, it cannot be kept waiting.

Ingredients:

Zest of 1 orange, very finely chopped, blanched, refreshed and well drained

1 quantity Mayonnaise (page 43), made with 1 tbsp lemon juice and 1 tbsp orange juice (no vinegar)

2 egg whites

Salt and paprika or cayenne

Serves 6

Preparation time: 5 minutes

Whisk the orange zest into the mayonnaise and add paprika or cayenne, as you prefer. Beat the egg whites stiffly and firm them up with a pinch of salt, then delicately fold them into the mayonnaise. Serve the sauce immediately.

Bagnarotte Sauce

This sauce dates back to my days as chef to Mlle Cécile de Rothschild in Paris, and I still often serve it at The Waterside Inn, particularly with canapés in the summer. It is delicious with large pink prawns or crab, ripe cherry tomatoes or raw cauliflower florets. It must be served very cold.

Ingredients:

1 quantity Mayonnaise (page 43)

3 tbsp tomato ketchup

1 tsp worcestershire sauce

1 tbsp cognac

2 tbsp double cream

6 drops of tabasco

Juice of $1/2$ lemon

Salt and freshly ground pepper

Serves 6

Preparation time: 3 minutes

Put the mayonnaise in a bowl and mix in all the other ingredients with a whisk. Season to taste with salt and pepper and keep in the fridge until ready to use.

Gribiche Sauce

Gribiche sauce was one of those that I most often concocted during the 1960s when I was chef to Mlle Cécile de Rothschild. She requested this sauce incessantly; she adored it served with cold fish, crustaceans, shellfish, smoked trout and hard-boiled eggs – in fact, with almost everything.

Ingredients:

4 freshly cooked hard-boiled egg yolks
1 tsp strong Dijon mustard
250 ml groundnut oil
1 tbsp white wine vinegar
Whites of 2 of the hard-boiled eggs, coarsely chopped
30 g small capers, drained, and chopped if they are large
30 g cornichons, finely diced
2 tbsp finely snipped fines herbes, (page 10)
Salt and freshly ground pepper

Serves 6

Preparation time: 5 minutes

Put the egg yolks, mustard and a little salt and pepper in a mortar and crush with the pestle to make a smooth paste. Gradually trickle in half the oil, mixing with the pestle as you go to amalgamate it thoroughly. Still mixing, add the vinegar, then continue to trickle in the remaining oil in the same way as before. Finally, add all the other ingredients, mix them in with a spoon and season the sauce to taste with salt and pepper.

Swedish Sauce

This sauce makes a good accompaniment to cold roast goose or pork, or to any thinly sliced cold smoked meats.

Ingredients:

200 g tart dessert apples, peeled, cored and cut into chunks
50 ml dry white wine
1 quantity Mayonnaise (page 43)
1 tbsp freshly grated horseradish
Salt and freshly ground pepper

Serves 6
Preparation time: 10 minutes
Cooking time: about 20 minutes

Put the apples and white wine in a saucepan, cover and cook over low heat for 15 – 20 minutes, until the apples are soft enough to be crushed with a fork. Turn off the heat and rub the apples through a sieve into a bowl. Reserve them in a cool place.

As soon as the apples are cold, mix them into the mayonnaise together with the horseradish, then season the sauce with salt and pepper.

Sea Urchin Sauce

Accentuate the flavour of cold crustaceans such as lobster, crab, spider crab or langoustines with this delicate sauce.

Ingredients:

Corals of 12 sea urchins (cut them open with scissor tips and scrape out the corals with a teaspoon)
1 quantity Mayonnaise (page 43)
1 tbsp Napoléon mandarine liqueur or grand marnier
100 ml whipping cream, whipped to a ribbon consistency
6 drops of tabasco
Salt

Serves 4
Preparation time: 5 minutes

Rub the sea urchin corals through a fine sieve, then fold them into the mayonnaise with a whisk. Delicately fold in the other ingredients with a spatula and season the sauce with salt.

Tartare Sauce

Tartare sauce is a classic which is used mainly to accompany any cold cooked fish.

Serves 6

Preparation time: 5 minutes

Ingredients:

3 hard-boiled egg yolks,
at room temperature
200 ml groundnut oil
1 tbsp wine vinegar or lemon juice
20 g onion, finely chopped, blanched,
refreshed and well drained
3 tbsp Mayonnaise (page 43)
1 tbsp snipped chives
Salt and freshly ground pepper

Put the egg yolks in a mortar and pound with the pestle to make a smooth paste (1). Season with salt and pepper, then incorporate the oil in a thin stream, stirring continuously with the pestle (2). When it is all incorporated and the sauce is smooth (3), add the vinegar or lemon juice, then the onion, chives and mayonnaise (4) and season to taste.

Rouille

Rouille is traditionally served with fish or mussel soup and bouillabaisse. Hand it round separately in a sauceboat or small olive wood bowl. If you are a garlic lover, crush an extra clove and add it to the finished sauce.

Ingredients:

250 g potatoes, peeled and steamed or boiled until tender, then drained

1 garlic clove

3 hard-boiled egg yolks

250 ml olive oil

A pinch of saffron

Fine salt and freshly ground white pepper

Serves 6

Preparation time: **5 minutes**

Put the drained potatoes back into the pan and toss around over medium heat to dry them out, or do this in the oven preheated to 180°C/350°F/gas mark 4.

Peel the garlic clove and roll it in fine salt, then rub it round the inside of a bowl. Rub first the potatoes, then the hard-boiled egg yolks through a fine sieve into the bowl. Stir with a spatula until well mixed, then blend in the olive oil, stirring continuously until very smooth. Season with salt and white pepper and finally add the saffron.

Mint-flavoured Cheese Coulis

This creamy, refreshing coulis is superb served with smoked salmon. I love to serve this dish for breakfast. You can use either full-fat or low-fat fromage frais.

Ingredients:

120 g fromage frais

180 ml milk

4 tbsp mint leaves

200 g cucumber, peeled, deseeded and finely diced

Salt and freshly ground pepper

Serves 8

Preparation time: **5 minutes**

Put the fromage frais, milk and mint leaves in a blender and whizz until smooth. Season to taste, then strain the coulis through a fine-mesh conical sieve and refrigerate.

Just before serving, sprinkle on the diced cucumber.

Maître d'Hôtel Butter

This classic topping remains a favourite for grilled meat or fish.

Ingredients:

150 g butter, softened
20 g parsley, snipped
Juice of 1/2 lemon
Salt and a pinch of cayenne pepper or
freshly ground black pepper

Makes about 175 g

Preparation time: **5 minutes**

Using a wooden spoon, work the parsley into the butter, then mix in the lemon juice. Season to taste and, using cling film, roll the butter into one or two sausage shapes. Refrigerate or freeze until needed.

Snail Butter

Snail butter is well known as an indispensable and inseparable accompaniment to snails. Sauté them in the hot prepared butter and serve as a first course. The nuts add a special flavour and bite.

Ingredients:

6 shelled hazelnuts
250 g butter, softened
2 large garlic cloves
1/2 very small shallot
6 tbsp snipped parsley
1 small pinch of nutmeg
Salt and freshly ground black pepper

Makes about 250 g

Preparation time: **15 minutes**

Preheat the oven or grill to very hot. Put the hazelnuts in the grill pan, place in the hot oven or under the grill for a few minutes, then rub with a cloth to remove the skins. Finely chop the nuts and reserve them.

Work the softened butter with a wooden spatula until creamy. Peel the garlic and shallot and chop very finely, then stir them into the butter together with the parsley and the finely chopped hazelnuts.

Using a spatula, work all the ingredients into the butter until thoroughly amalgamated, then season with nutmeg, pepper and 1 teaspoon salt. Refrigerate or freeze until ready to use.

Goat's Cheese Butter

Discs of goat's cheese butter make an appetizing topping for grilled white meats, like veal escalopes or chicken wings. The butter is also delicious with pasta; mix it in just before serving and add a little snipped basil or flat-leaf parsley to enhance the flavour of the cheesy butter.

Makes about 300 g

*Preparation time: **5 minutes***

Ingredients:

150 g fresh or semi-hard goat's cheese, whichever you prefer

150 g butter, softened

Cut up the goat's cheese, put it in a mortar or food processor with the butter (1) and pound with a pestle (2) or process for about 3 minutes, scraping the butter and cheese towards the centre of the bowl every minute to obtain a completely homogeneous mixture. Using a plastic scraper, rub the flavoured butter through a drum sieve to eliminate any hard grains of cheese (3), then put it on a sheet of cling film (4). Roll the butter into one or two sausage shapes (5). Refrigerate or freeze until ready to use.

Roquefort Butter

Use this butter as a delicious spread for toast canapés, or whisk it into a fish velouté to add extra character and piquancy. This is particularly good with cooked shelled mussels served in ramekins. A tablespoon of roquefort butter added to a sauce for poultry is also surprisingly good.

Ingredients:

150 g butter, softened
100 g roquefort
Freshly ground pepper

Makes 250 g

Preparation time: 5 minutes

Crumble the roquefort and work it into the softened butter with a wooden spoon. Using a plastic scraper, rub it through a drum sieve and season with pepper. Using cling film, roll the butter into one or two sausage shapes and refrigerate or freeze until ready to use.

Caviar Butter

Serve this flavoursome, delicate butter in a sauceboat to accompany grilled fillets of sole or John Dory. It is best to use it on the day it is made, without refrigerating or freezing it.

Ingredients:

60 g caviar, preferably pressed
(otherwise use sevruga)
150 g butter, softened
Salt and freshly ground pepper

Makes about 200 g

Preparation time: 5 minutes

Using a wooden spoon, mix the caviar into the butter, then, using a plastic scraper, rub it through a drum sieve. Season to taste and use on the same day.

Red Pepper Butter

Like anchovy butter, red pepper butter is excellent spread on toast canapés, and accompanies poached fish extremely well. Whisked into white or hot emulsion sauces, this butter will enhance the flavour and colour and add a touch of originality.

Makes about 200 g
Preparation time: 5 minutes
Cooking time: 5 minutes

Ingredients:

170 g butter, softened
60 g red pepper, finely diced
1 sprig of thyme
Salt and freshly ground black pepper

Melt 20 g butter in a small saucepan and add the diced pepper and thyme. Sweat gently for 5 minutes, then leave at room temperature until cold. Mix the cooked red pepper into the remaining softened butter with a wooden spoon, then use a plastic scraper to rub the butter through a drum sieve or whizz in a blender. Using cling film, roll the butter into one or two sausage shapes and refrigerate or freeze until ready to use.

Vegetable Butter

This butter will lift a white sauce out of the ordinary with its special flavour and perfect colour. A few discs make a most delicious topping for boiled potatoes (picture, page 9).

Ingredients:

150 g vegetables of your choice, e.g.
carrots, french beans or asparagus
150 g butter, softened

Makes about 260 g

Preparation time: *10 minutes*

Cooking time: *about 5 minutes*

Peel or trim and wash the vegetables and cook them in lightly salted water until tender. Refresh, drain and pat dry with a cloth.

Put the cooked vegetables and the butter in a food processor and whizz for about 3 minutes, scraping the ingredients into the centre of the bowl every minute to make a homogeneous mixture. If you don't have a food processor, use a pestle and mortar.

Using a plastic scraper, rub the flavoured butter through a drum sieve to eliminate any vegetable fibres. Using cling film, roll it into one or two sausage shapes and refrigerate or freeze until ready to use.

Foie Gras Butter

This creamy, delicate and tasty butter is excellent on toast canapés. A few discs add a wonderful flavour to a grilled steak, but best of all, it gives a superb velvety, unctuous finish to many sauces for meat, poultry and game.

Ingredients:

100 g butter, softened
100 g terrine or ballotine of duck or
goose foie gras
2 tbsp armagnac or cognac
Salt and freshly ground pepper

Makes about 200 g

Preparation time: *5 minutes*

Mix all the ingredients with a wooden spoon, seasoning to taste with salt and pepper. Using a plastic scraper, rub through a drum sieve or whizz in a blender. Using cling film, roll the butter into one or two sausage shapes and refrigerate or freeze until needed.

Paprika Butter

This butter is perfect served with grilled escalopes of veal, turkey or chicken.

Ingredients:

20 g butter
30 g onion, finely chopped
150 g butter, softened
$1/2$ – 1 tbsp paprika, according to taste
Salt and freshly ground pepper

Makes about 180 g
Preparation time: 10 minutes

Melt the 20 g butter in a small saucepan, add the onion and sweat gently for 2 minutes. Leave to cool and, as soon as the onion is completely cold, mix it into the softened butter with a wooden spoon. Add the paprika and season to taste with salt and pepper. Using a plastic scraper, rub the flavoured butter through a sieve or whizz in a food processor. Using cling film, roll it into one or two sausage shapes and refrigerate or freeze until needed.

Curry Butter: This can be made in the same way; just double the quantity of onion and the butter to sweat it in, and replace the paprika with 1 – 2 tablespoons curry powder, according to taste. Add the curry to the onions after 1 minute, not directly to the softened butter. Curry butter can be used with the same meats as paprika butter, and also with grilled pork chops.

Crab Butter

Serve crab butter on toast canapés, or use it to add extra body to sauces for scallops and seafood.

Ingredients:

150 g of the yellowish-grey meat
from inside a crab shell
150 g butter, softened
1 tbsp cognac
1 tsp harissa, or 5 drops of tabasco
Juice of $1/2$ lemon
Salt and freshly ground pepper

Makes about 300 g
Preparation time: 7 minutes

Whizz the crab meat and butter in a blender for 3 minutes. Rub through a drum sieve then, with a wooden spoon, mix in the cognac, harissa or tabasco and the lemon juice and season. Using cling film, roll the butter into one or two sausage shapes and refrigerate or freeze until needed.

Chilled Vegetable Coulis

These chilled vegetable coulis make excellent accompaniments to cold poached fish served as part of a buffet, or by themselves as a summer hors d'oeuvre. I sometimes serve three different coulis (carrot, celeriac and pea, for example) as an attractive, mellow amuse-gueule, placing a tablespoon of each on a small plate, to be eaten with a teaspoon.

Ingredients:

360 g carrots or celeriac, peeled and diced, or
360 g french beans, or 500 g shelled fresh peas
500 ml double cream
Salt and freshly ground pepper

Serves 6

Preparation time: 10 minutes

Cooking time: 5 – 20 minutes, depending on the vegetables

Cook your chosen vegetable in boiling salted water until tender. Drain and whizz in a blender with 100 ml cream to make a very smooth purée. Transfer to a bowl and leave to cool, stirring from time to time. Using a whisk, gently stir in the rest of the cream. Season the coulis to taste with salt and pepper and chill in the fridge until needed.

Raw Tomato Coulis

I adore this coulis served with cold poached eggs or as a sauce for cold pasta – a simple, refreshing summer dish which is very quick to prepare.

Ingredients:

350 g very ripe tomatoes, puréed then rubbed through a sieve to give about 250 ml juice and pulp
60 ml sherry vinegar (preferably), or balsamic vinegar
8 coriander seeds, crushed
12 basil leaves, shredded
1 tsp tomato purée (optional)
100 ml olive oil
Salt and freshly ground pepper

Serves 6

Preparation time: 5 minutes

Put all the ingredients in a bowl, except the basil leaves. Mix with a whisk, season with salt and pepper, then add the basil. The coulis is ready to serve. Alternatively, transfer it to an airtight container and refrigerate; it will keep well for 3 days.

ndex

Index

Acknowledgements

This edition published in 2000 by
Quadrille Publishing Ltd
Alhambra House
27 – 31 Charing Cross Road
London WC2H 0LS

Based on material originally published
in *Sauces; sweet and savoury, classic
and new* by Michel Roux.

Text © 1996 & 2000 Michel Roux
Photography © 1996 & 2000
Martin Brigdale
Design & layout © 2000
Quadrille Publishing Ltd

Publishing director: **Anne Furniss**
Art Director: **Mary Evans**
Art Editor: **Rachel Gibson**
Project editor & translator: **Kate Whiteman**
Editorial Assistant: **Caroline Perkins**
Styling: **Helen Trent**
Production: **Rachel Wells**

The right of Michel Roux to be identified as
the Author of this Work has been asserted
him in accordance with the Copyright,
Designs and Patents Act 1988.

The publisher would like to thank Divertimen
for supplying the kitchenware for photograp

Cataloguing-in-Publication Data: a catalog
record for this book is available from the
British Library.

ISBN 1 902757 41 6

Printed & bound by Dai Nippon Printing
Company Ltd, Hong Kong